M000074009

Published by Barbour Publishing, Inc., P.O. Box 719, Uhrichsville, Ohio 44683
http://www.barbourbooks.com

Member of the
Evangelical Christian
Publishers Association

Printed in the United States of America.

Let Freedom Ring

CATHY MARIE HAKE AND DEBORAH BOONE

BARBOUR
PUBLISHING, INC.
Uhrichsville, Ohio

. . .proclaim liberty throughout all the land to all its inhabitants.
LEVITICUS 25:10 (*INSCRIPTION ON THE LIBERTY BELL*)

America

MY country 'tis of thee,
Sweet land of liberty,
Of thee I sing:
Land where my fathers died,
Land of the pilgrims' pride,
From every mountain side
Let freedom ring.

Our fathers' God, to Thee,
Author of liberty,
To Thee we sing;
Long may our land be bright
With freedom's holy light;
Protect us by Thy might,
Great God, our King!

SAMUEL FRANCIS SMITH

Let Freedom Ring

Below her spacious sapphire skies,
Above the cliffs where eagle flies,
Far from the bounds of earthly care,
A cadence rises through the air.

Upon her fields once stained with red,
Beneath the tombs of heroes dead,
Beats a pulse with fervor fine—
A gift from heaven most divine.

Within her countless hallowed halls,
Beyond mere confine of all walls,
There moves a spirit ere unseen,
Yet felt with every heartbeat keen.

God's own grace upon this land,
Foundations built by mighty hand,
Her tenor soars on eagle's wing,
From sea to sea let freedom ring!

KATHI KOLOSIEKE

5

Righteousness exalts a nation...

PROVERBS 14:34

The more profoundly we study
this wonderful Book,
and the more closely
we observe its divine precepts,
the better citizens we will become
and the higher will be
our destiny as a nation.

WILLIAM MCKINLEY

Whatever makes men good Christians,
makes them good citizens.

DANIEL WEBSTER

. . .Those duties are to God,
to your fellow creatures, and to yourself.
"Thou shalt love the Lord thy God,
with all thy heart,
and with all thy soul,
and with all thy mind,
and with all thy strength,
and thy neighbor as yourself."

JOHN QUINCY ADAMS

A patriot without religion in my estimation is as great a paradox
as an honest man without the fear of God.

ABIGAIL ADAMS

The God who made the world
and everything in it
is the Lord of heaven and earth. . . .
he himself gives all men life and breath
and everything else.

ACTS 17:24–25

Thank You, Lord, for Your faithfulness
to all generations—
for Your goodness and mercy
to those who seek Your face.

Every good and perfect gift is from above,
coming down from the Father of the heavenly lights,
who does not change like shifting shadows.

JAMES 1:17

We hold these truths to be self-evident;
that all men are created equal;
that they are endowed by their Creator
with certain inalienable Rights; that among these are
Life, Liberty, and the pursuit of Happiness;
that to secure these rights, governments
are instituted among men,
deriving their just powers
from the consent of the governed.

THOMAS JEFFERSON
THE DECLARATION OF INDEPENDENCE,
JULY 4, 1776

After the signing of the Declaration of Independence,
Samuel Adams commented:

"We have this day restored the Sovereign to whom all men
ought to be obedient. He reigns in heaven and from the rising
to the setting of the sun, let His Kingdom come."

So great is my veneration of the Bible,
that the earlier my children begin to read it
the more confident will be my hope that they
will prove useful citizens of their country
and respectable members of society.

JOHN QUINCY ADAMS

The Bible is endorsed by the ages;
our civilization is built upon its words.
In no other book is there such a collection
of inspired wisdom, reality and hope.

DWIGHT D. EISENHOWER

Within the covers of the Bible
are all the answers
for all the problems men face.
The Bible can touch hearts,
order minds, and refresh souls.

RONALD REAGAN

There are a good many problems
before the American people today
and before me as president,
but I expect to find the solution
of those problems just in the proportion
that I am faithful in the study
of the word of God.

WOODROW WILSON

EVeryone must submit himself
to the governing authorities,
for there is no authority
except that which God has established.
The authorities that exist
have been established by God.
Consequently, he who rebels against authority
is rebelling against what God has instituted,
and those who do so bring judgment on themselves.

ROMANS 13:1–2

I urge, then, first of all, that requests, prayers,
intercession and thanksgiving be made for everyone—
for kings and all those in authority, that we may live peaceful
and quiet lives in all godliness and holiness.

1 TIMOTHY 2:1–2

God who gave us life gave us liberty.
And can the liberties of a nation be thought secure
when we have removed their only firm basis,
a conviction in the minds of the people
that these liberties
are the gift of God?

THOMAS JEFFERSON

We the people of the United States,
in order to form a more perfect Union,
establish Justice, insure domestic Tranquility,
provide for the common defense, promote the general Welfare,
and secure the Blessings of Liberty to ourselves and our Posterity,
do ordain and establish this Constitution
of the United States of America.

PREAMBLE TO THE
CONSTITUTION OF THE UNITED STATES

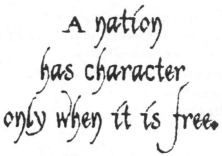

A nation has character only when it is free.

MADAME DE STAEL

Tyranny is so generally established in the rest of the world that the prospect of an asylum in America for those who love liberty gives general joy, and our cause is esteemed the cause of all mankind. . . . We are fighting for the dignity and happiness of human nature. Glorious it is for the Americans to be called by Providence to this post of honor. Cursed and detested will everyone be that deserts or betrays it.

BENJAMIN FRANKLIN

A MIGHTY woman with a torch,
whose flame. . .
From her beacon hand
Glows worldwide welcome. . .
"Give me your tired, your poor,
your huddled masses
yearning to breathe free. . . ."

EMMA LAZARUS
QUOTE AT THE BASE OF THE STATUE OF LIBERTY

just as the statue of Liberty welcomes those

seeking a new life, christ invites

and welcomes us into new life.

It is for freedom that christ has set us free.

GALATIANS 5:1

The religion which has introduced civil liberty is the religion of Christ and His Apostles. . . . This is genuine Christianity, and to this we owe our free constitutions of government.

NOAH WEBSTER

NOW the Lord is the Spirit, and
where the Spirit of the Lord is,
there is freedom.

2 CORINTHIANS 3:17

It is extremely important to our nation, in a political as
well as religious view, that all possible authority and influ-
ence should be given to the Scriptures, for these furnish
the best principles of civil liberty, and the most effectual
support of republican government. The principles of all
genuine liberty, and of wise laws and administrations are
to be drawn from the Bible and sustained by its authority.
The man therefore who weakens or destroys the divine
authority of that book may be accessory to all the public
disorders which society is doomed to suffer. . . .

NOAH WEBSTER

We identify the flag with almost everything we hold dear on earth. It represents our peace and security, our civil and political liberty, our freedom of religious worship, our family, our friends, our home. We see it in the great multitude of blessings, of rights and privileges that make up our country.

But when we look at our flag and behold it emblazoned with all our rights, we must remember that it is equally a symbol of our duties. Every glory that we associate with it is the result of duty done.

CALVIN COOLIDGE

The pledge of Allegiance

"I pledge allegiance to the flag
of the United States of America
and to the Republic for which it stands,
one Nation under God, indivisible,
with liberty and justice for all."

IN this way we are reaffirming the transcendence of religious faith in America's heritage and future; in this way we shall constantly strengthen those spiritual weapons which forever will be our country's most powerful resource in peace and war.

DWIGHT D. EISENHOWER,
IN A 1954 SPEECH AFTER CONGRESS
AMENDED THE PLEDGE OF ALLEGIANCE
TO ADD THE WORDS "UNDER GOD."

Our Flag carries American ideas,
American history
and American feelings.
Beginning with the Colonies,
and coming down to our time,
in its sacred heraldry, in its glorious insignia,
it has gathered and stored chiefly this supreme idea:
divine right of liberty in man.
Every color means liberty;
every thread means liberty;
every form of star and beam
or stripe of light means liberty—
not lawlessness, but organized,
institutional liberty—
liberty through law, and laws for liberty!

HENRY WARD BEECHER

stars, stripes, and sacrifice

The thirteen stripes not only represent the original thirteen colonies that conceived the notion of our freedom, their colors honor our country's greatest men. From basic liberties to sweet justice, etched in those white lines lies the promise of our nation. The lifeblood spilled by our armed forces is mourned in broad red steams across this most recognized badge of American splendor. Every freedom we have shines there, sandwiched between crimson lines of sacrifice.

Our forefathers designated the white stars on a blue field to "represent a new constellation," such as those God placed in the heavens. Together, we create the living legend that a government based on tolerance and freedom can succeed. As the stars draw our eyes toward our heavenly Father, so too American freedom sets the course for other nations.

KELLY HAKE

A thoughtful mind,
when it sees a Nation's flag,
sees not the flag only,
but the nation itself. . .
the history which belongs
to the Nation that it sets forth.

HENRY WARD BEECHER

Our brightest hope for the future flutters from the flag posts of our schools, and we give no greater tribute than a flag-draped bier. The promise of tomorrow and our gratitude for the past are woven

in red's valor,

white's purity,

and blue's limitless horizon.

Star Spangled Banner

O say can you see by the dawn's early light,
What so proudly we hailed at the twilight's last gleaming,
Whose broad stripes and bright stars through the perilous fight,
O'er the ramparts we watch'd, were so gallantly streaming?
And the Rockets' red glare, the Bombs bursting in air,
Gave proof through the night that our Flag was still there;
O! say does that star-spangled Banner yet wave,
O'er the Land of the free, and the home of the brave?

O! thus be it ever when freemen shall stand,
Between their lov'd home, and the war's desolation,
blest with vict'ry and peace, may the Heav'n rescued land,
Praise the Power that hath made and preserv'd us a nation!
Then conquer we must, when our cause it is just,
And this be our motto—"In God is our Trust."

FRANCIS SCOTT KEY

T**he** Bible must be considered as the great source of all the truth
by which men are to be guided in government as well
as in all social transactions. . . .

NOAH WEBSTER

Blessed is the nation
whose god is the LORD.

PSALM 33:12

I**t** can not be emphasized too strongly or too often that this great
nation was founded, not by religionists, but by Christians,
not on religions, but on the gospel of Jesus Christ!

Patrick Henry

That Book, sir, is the rock
on which our republic rests.

ANDREW JACKSON

Belief in,
and
dependence on,
God
is absolutely
essential.

RONALD REAGAN

25

The Founding Fathers made an appropriate choice when they selected the bald eagle as the emblem of the nation. The fierce beauty and proud independence of this great bird aptly symbolize the strength and freedom of America.

JOHN F. KENNEDY

But those who wait on the LORD
will renew their strength.
They will soar on wings like eagles;
they will run and not grow weary,
they will walk and not be faint.

ISAIAH 40:31

The future doesn't belong
to the fainthearted;
it belongs to the brave.

RONALD REAGAN

Let every nation know,
whether it wishes us well or ill,
that we shall pay any price,
bear any burden, meet any hardship,
support any friend, oppose any foe,
in order to assure the survival
and the success of liberty.

JOHN F. KENNEDY

• • • the longer I live the more convincing proofs I see
of this truth, that God governs in the affairs of man. And
if a sparrow cannot fall to the ground without his notice,
is it probable that an empire can rise without his aid?

BENJAMIN FRANKLIN

Are not two sparrows
sold for a penny?
Yet not one of them will fall to the ground
apart from the will of your Father. . .
So don't be afraid;
you are worth more than many sparrows.

MATTHEW 10:29, 31

O Lord, how grateful I am for Your unfailing love—
for Your right hand that reaches down
to comfort me when I am afraid.

America is a nation full of good fortune, with so much to be grateful for. But we are not spared from suffering. In every generation, the world has produced enemies of human freedom. They have attacked America, because we are freedom's home and defender. And the commitment of our fathers is now the calling of our time.

GEORGE W. BUSH

Men must choose
to be governed by God,
or condemn themselves
to be ruled by tyrants.

WILLIAM PENN

Blandishments will not fascinate us, nor will the threats of a "halter" intimidate. For, under God, we are determined that whatsoever, whensoever, or howsoever we shall be called to make our exit, we shall die free men.

JOSIAH QUINCY

The
LORD
reigns
forever. . . . He will govern the peoples with
justice. Those who know your name will
trust
in you,
for you,
LORD
have
never
forsaken
those
who
seek
you.

PSALM 9:7–8, 10

Lord, let us come together to kneel before You
so our country will stand strong.

31

The American's Creed

"I believe in the United States of America as a Government of the people, by the people, for the people, whose just powers are derived from the consent of the governed; a democracy in a Republic; a sovereign Nation of many sovereign States; a perfect Union, one and inseparable; established upon those principles of freedom, equality, justice, and humanity for which American patriots sacrificed their lives and fortunes. I therefore believe it is my duty to my Country to love it; to support its Constitution; to obey its laws; to respect its flag, and to defend it against all enemies."

WILLIAM TYLER PAGE

Protection and patriotism are reciprocal.

JOHN C. CALHOUN

Whensoever hostile aggressions. . .require a resort to war, we must meet our duty and convince the world we are just friends and brave enemies.

THOMAS JEFFERSON

Greater love has no one than this, that he lay down his life for his friends.

JOHN 15:13

God grants liberty only to those who love it, and are always ready to guard and defend it.

DANIEL WEBSTER

• • •That this nation, under God, shall have a
new birth of freedom, and that Government
of the people, by the people, for the people,
shall not perish from the earth.

ABRAHAM LINCOLN

If my people, who are called by my name, will humble
themselves and pray and seek my face and turn from
their wicked ways, then will I hear from heaven and will
forgive their sin and will heal their land.

2 CHRONICLES 7:14

Freedom and fear, justice and cruelty,
have always been at war, and we know
that God is not neutral between them.

GEORGE W. BUSH

34

HOW priceless is your unfailing love!
Both high and low among men
find refuge in
the shadow of your wings.

PSALM 36:7

Regardless
of what goes on,
God
is ever faithful
and never changing.

O righteous God,
who searches minds and hearts,
bring to an end the violence
of the wicked
and make the
righteous secure.

PSALM 7:9

The only limit to our realization of tomorrow
will be our doubts of today.
Let us move forward
with strong and
active faith.

FRANKLIN D. ROOSEVELT

When justice is done,
it brings joy to the righteous,
but terror to evildoers.

PROVERBS 21:15

America, the Beautiful

O beautiful for spacious skies,
For amber waves of grain,
For purple mountain majesties
Above the fruited plain!
America! America!
God shed his grace on thee
And crown thy good with brotherhood
From sea to shining sea!

O beautiful for pilgrim feet,
Whose stern, impassioned stress
A thoroughfare for freedom beat
Across the wilderness!
America! America!
God mend thy every flaw,
Confirm thy soul in self-control,
Thy liberty in law!

O beautiful for heros proved
In liberating strife,
Who more than self their country loved,
And mercy more than life!
America! America!
May God thy gold refine,
Till all success be nobleness
And every gain divine!

O beautiful for patriot dream
That sees beyond the years
Thine alabaster cities gleam
Undimmed by human tears!
America! America!
God shed his grace on thee
And crown thy good with brotherhood
From sea to shining sea!

KATHARINE LEE BATES

We ask almighty god
to watch over our nation. . .
and may He always guide

our country.

GEORGE W. BUSH
SEPTEMBER 14, 2001